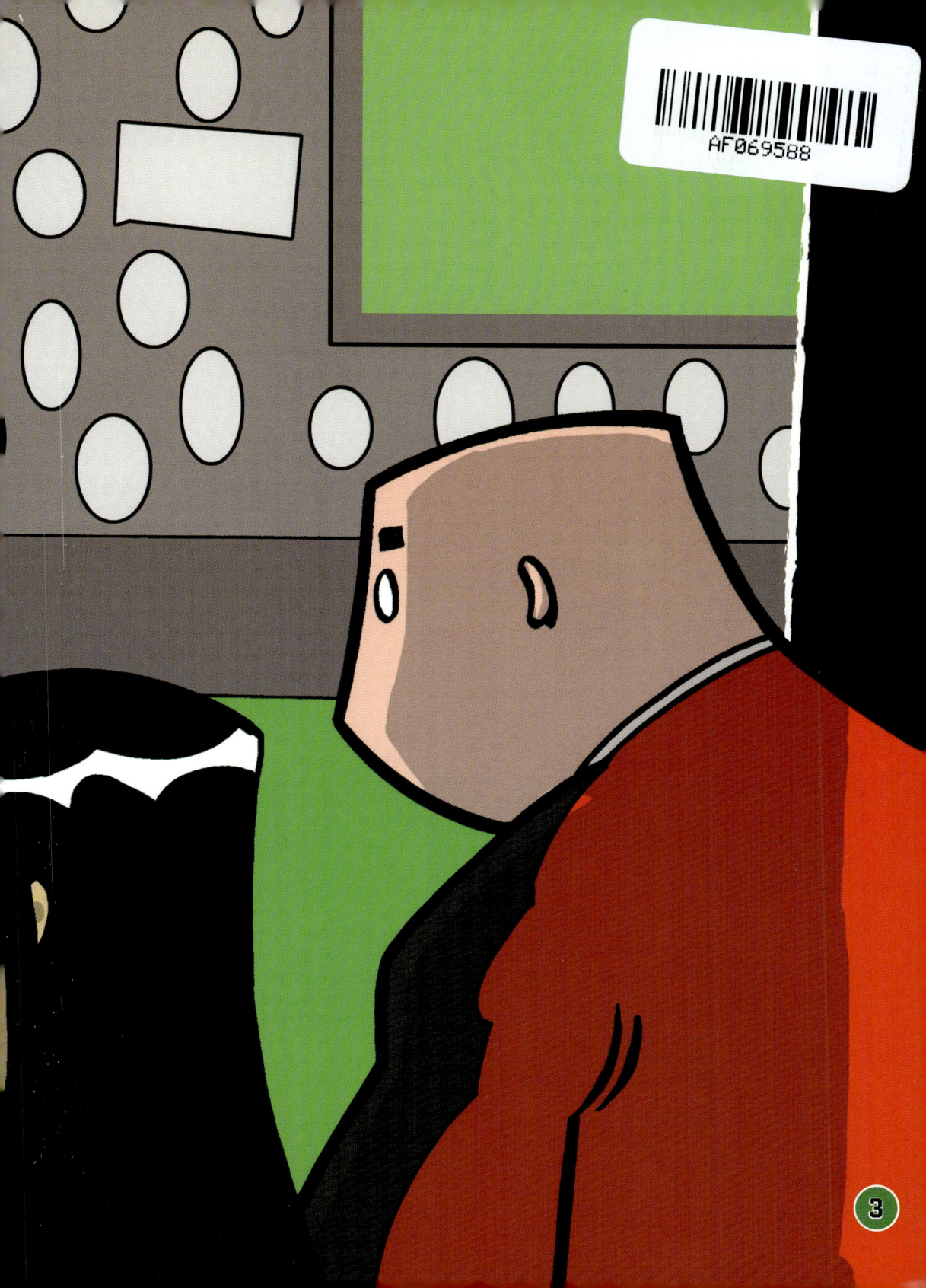

The match starts but without Art, Scooter and Janaki. They are not playing! They are on the bench. They are subs!

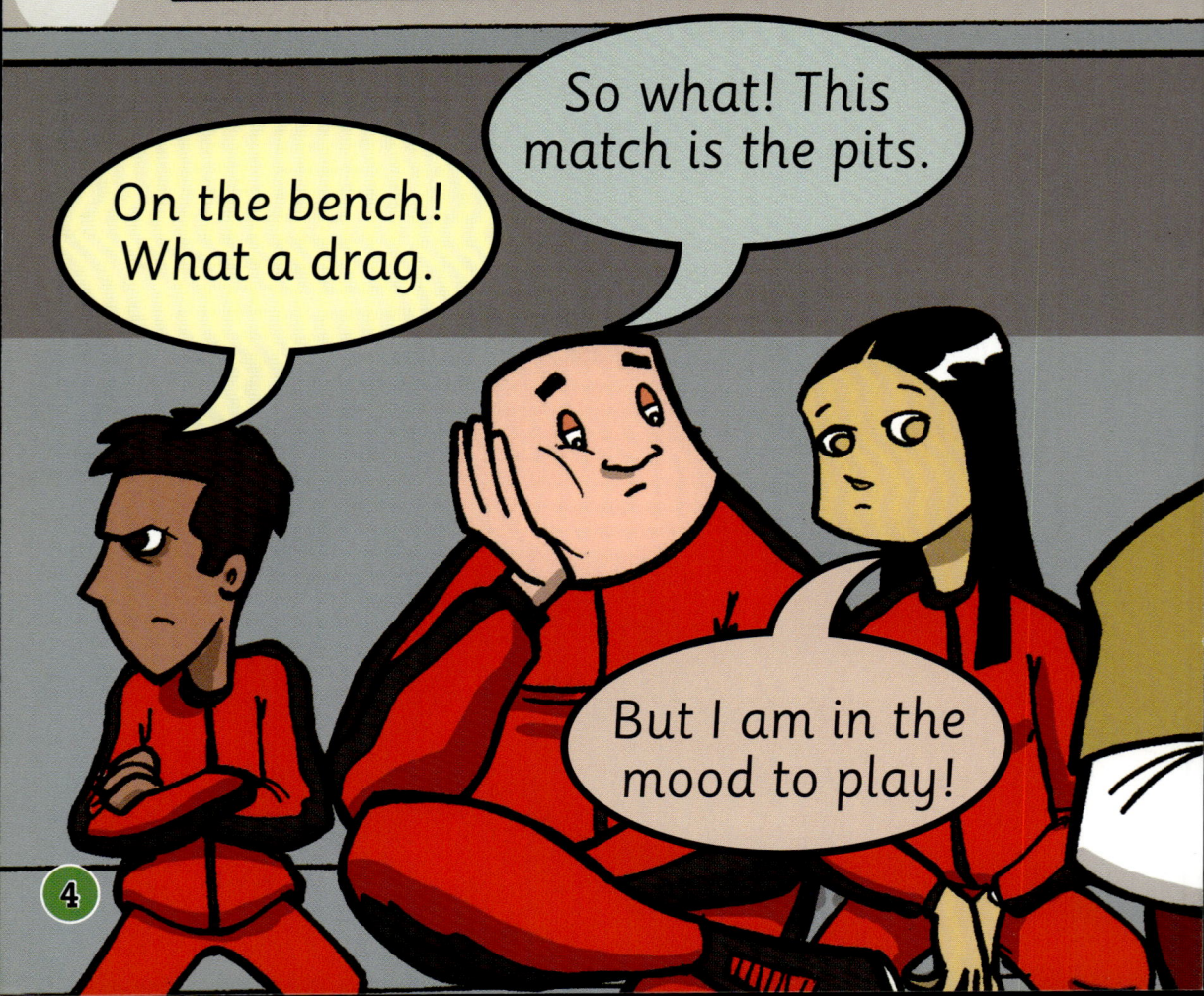

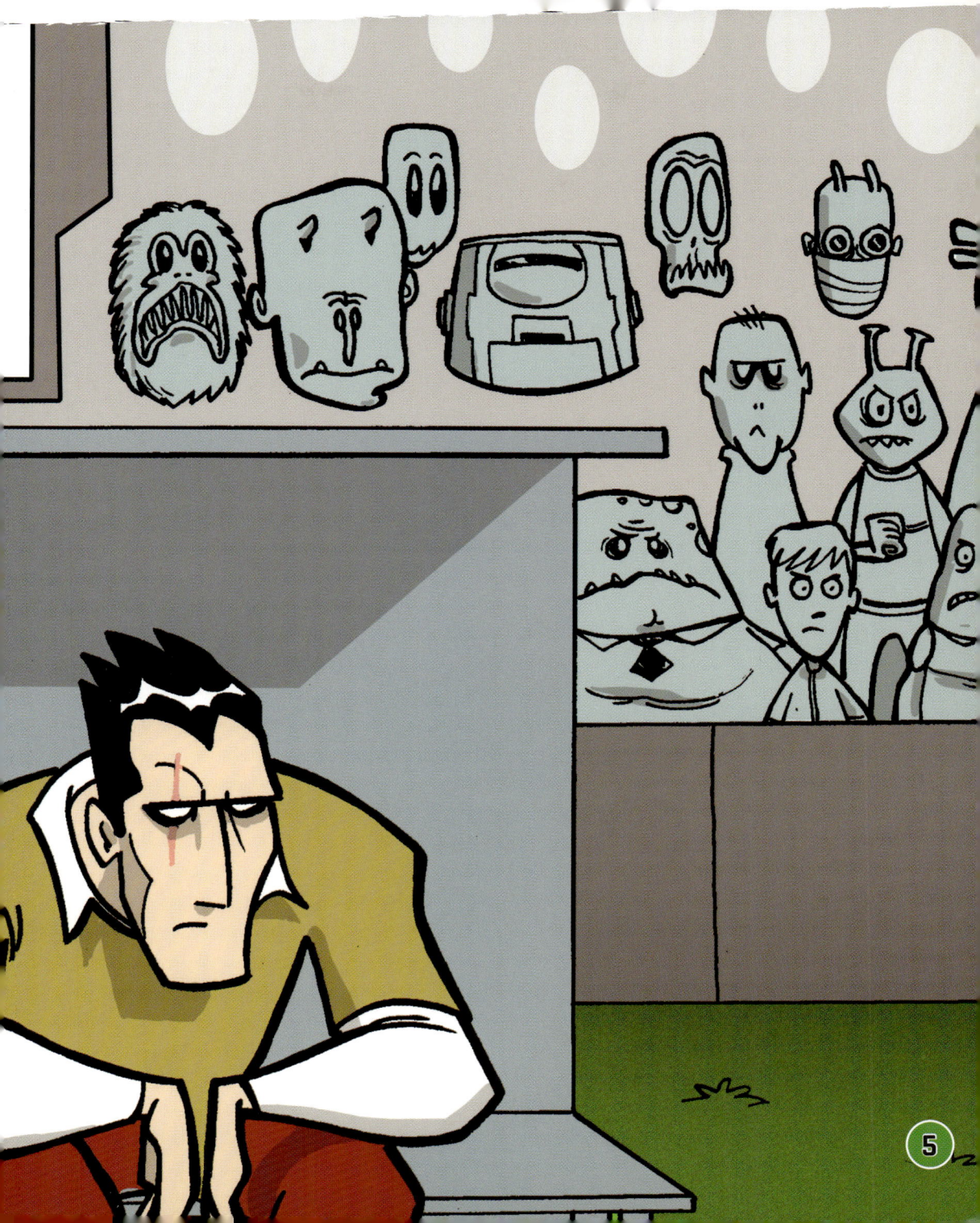

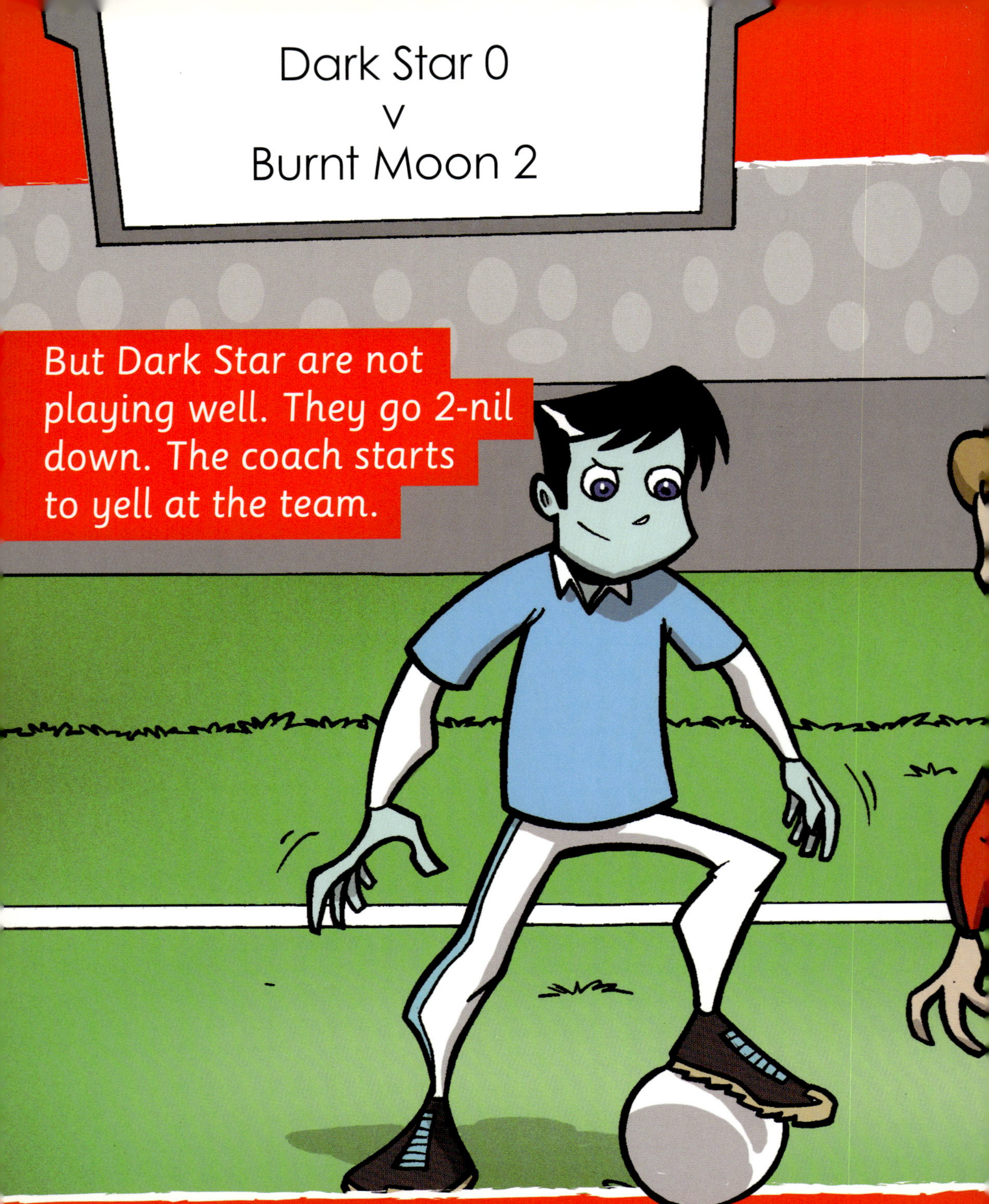

Dark Star 0
v
Burnt Moon 2

But Dark Star are not playing well. They go 2-nil down. The coach starts to yell at the team.

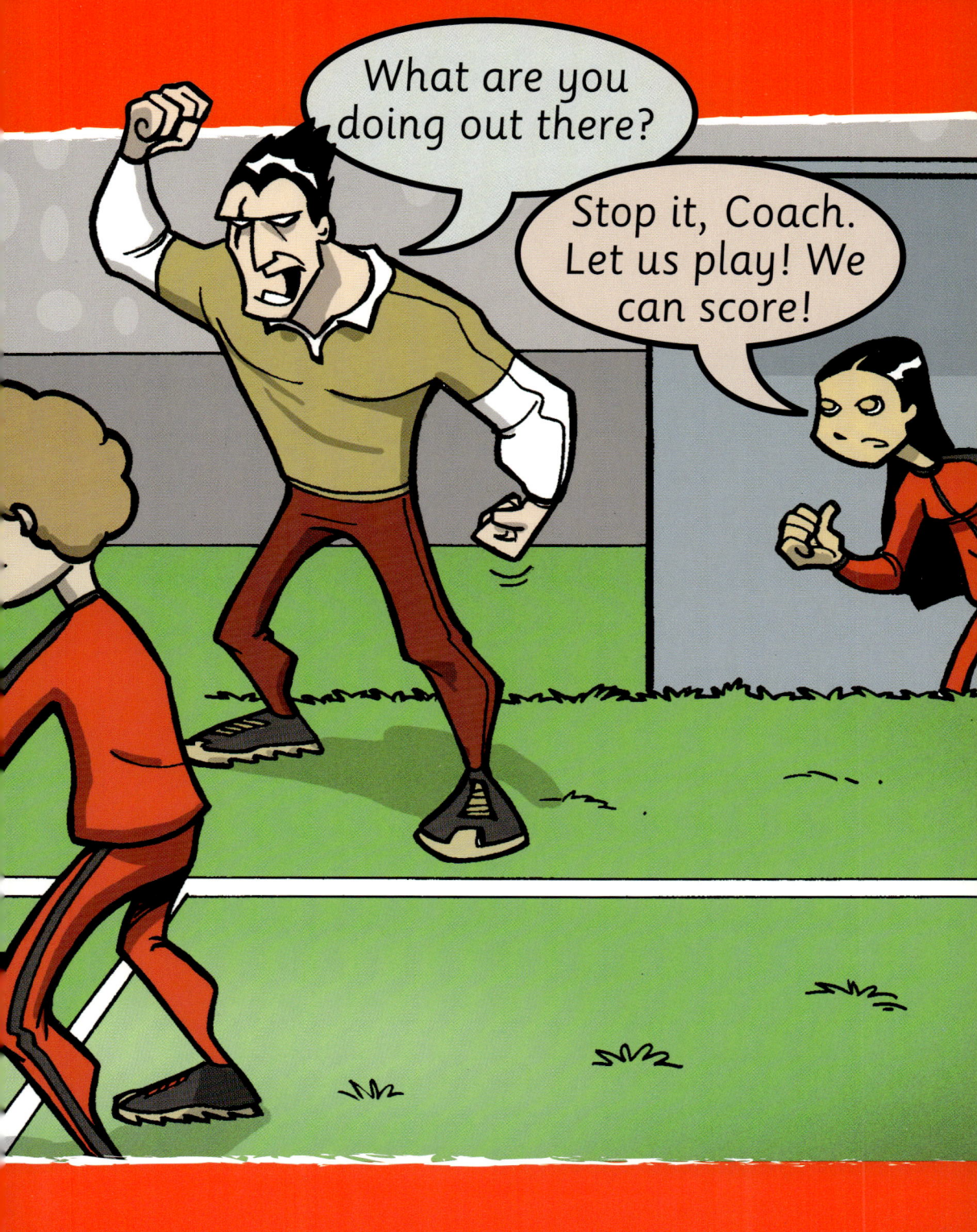

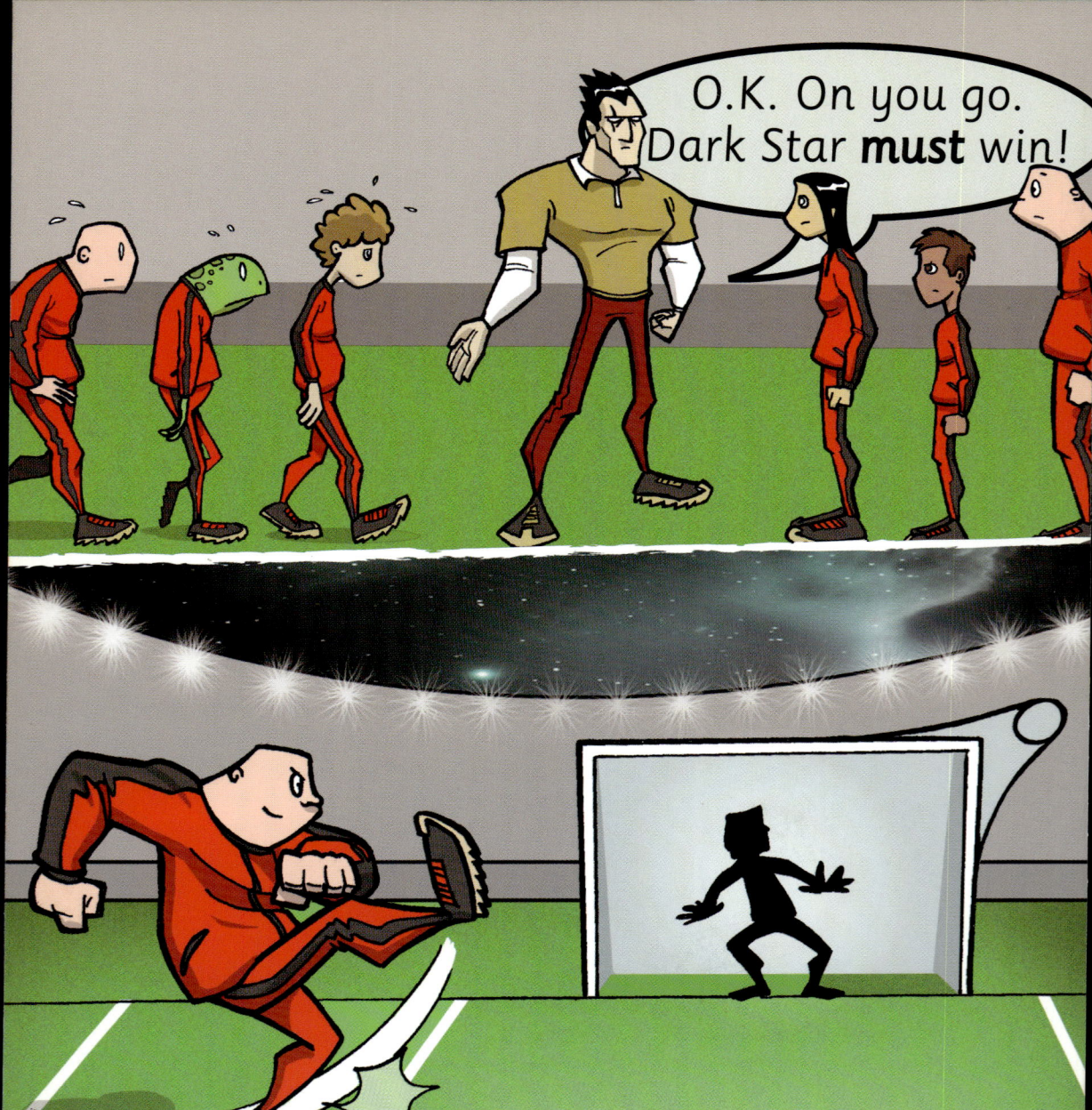

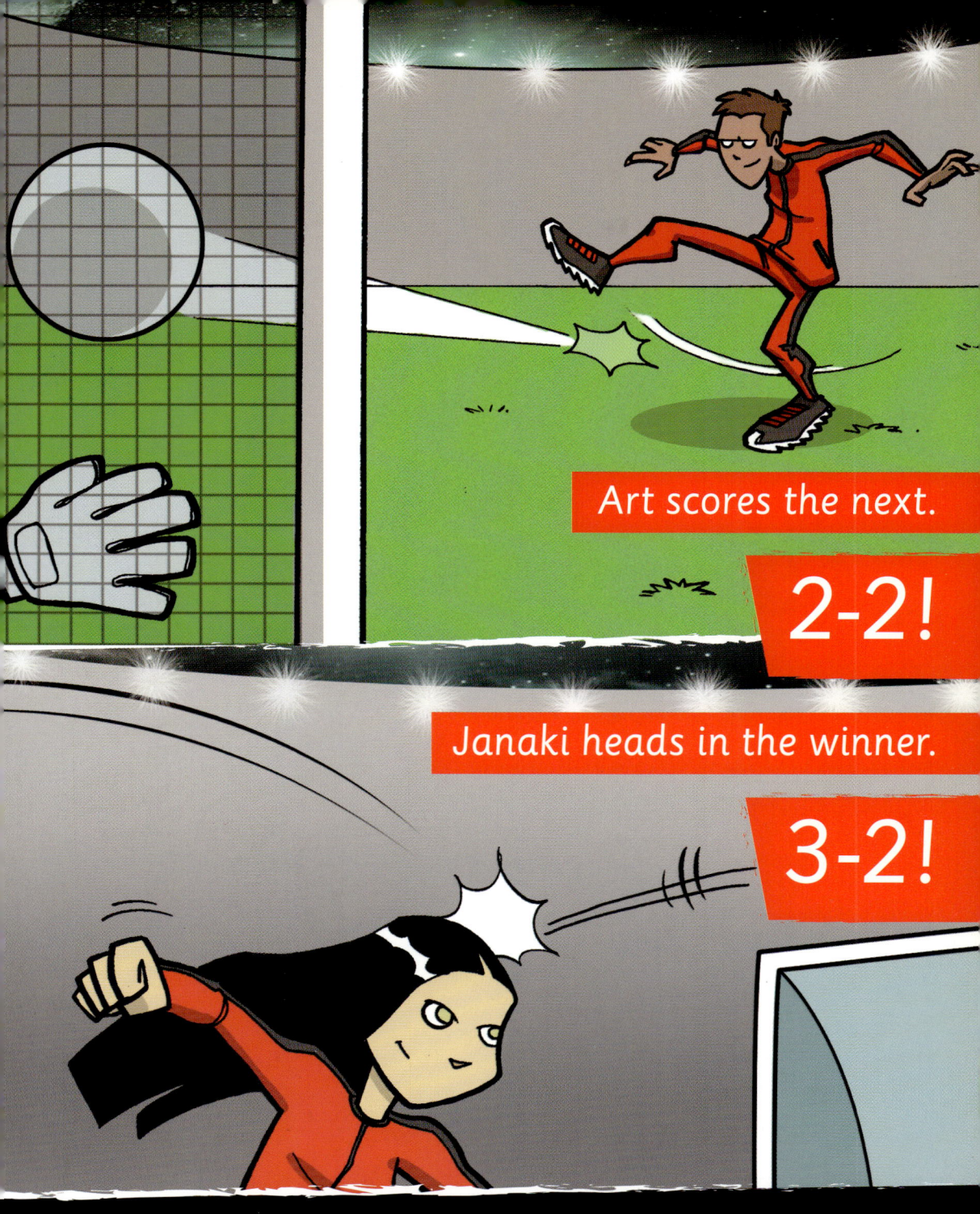

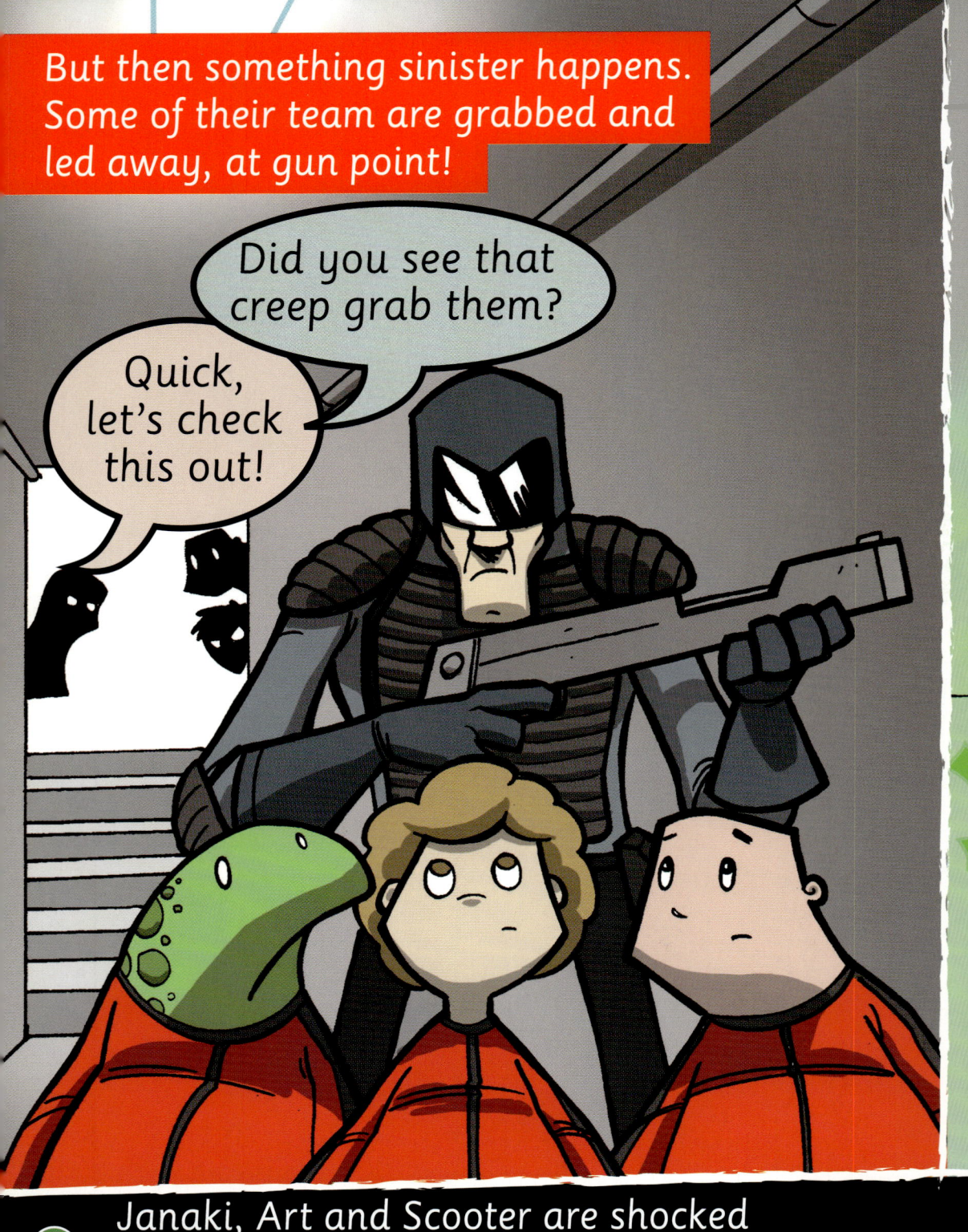

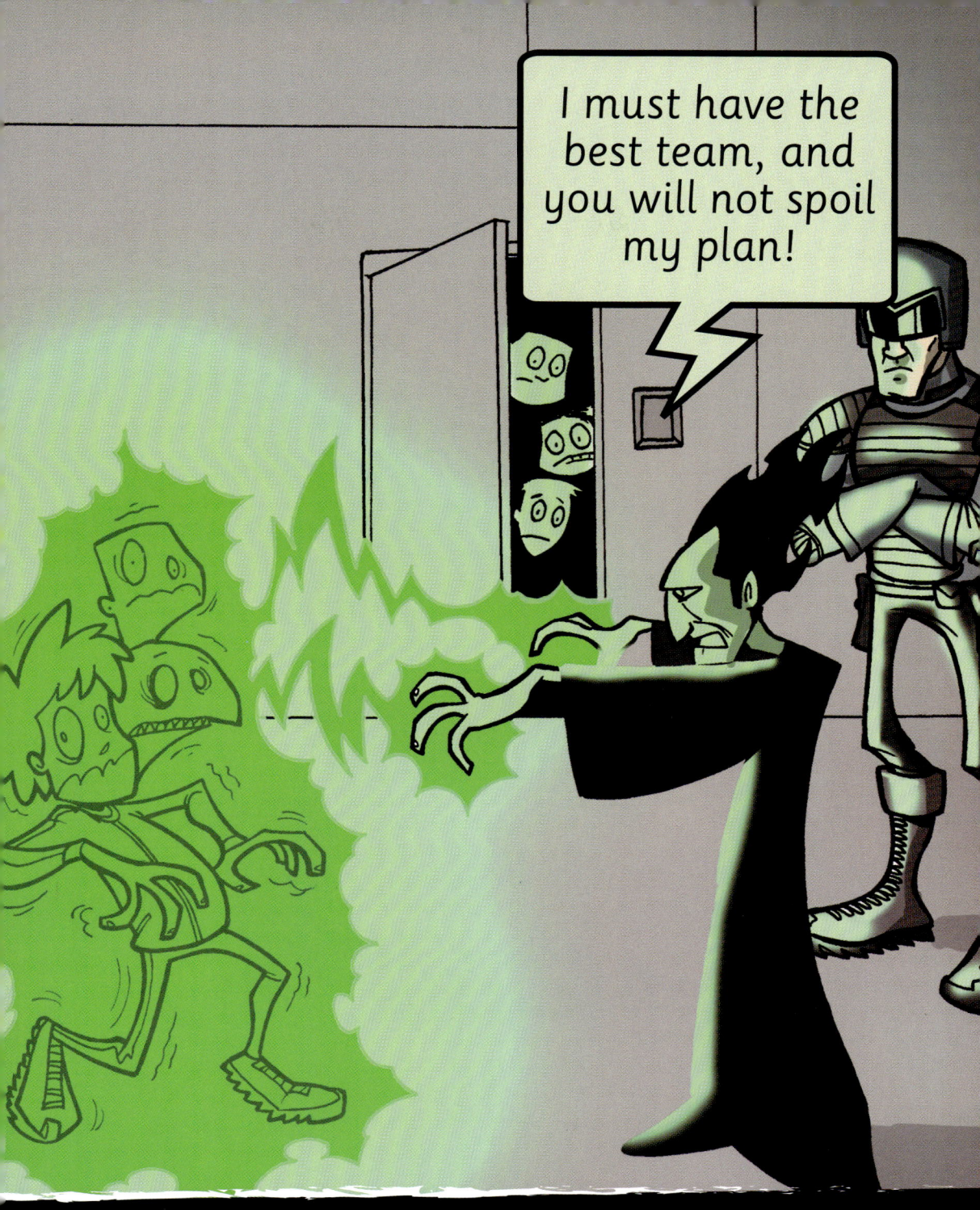

It is Zardoz!

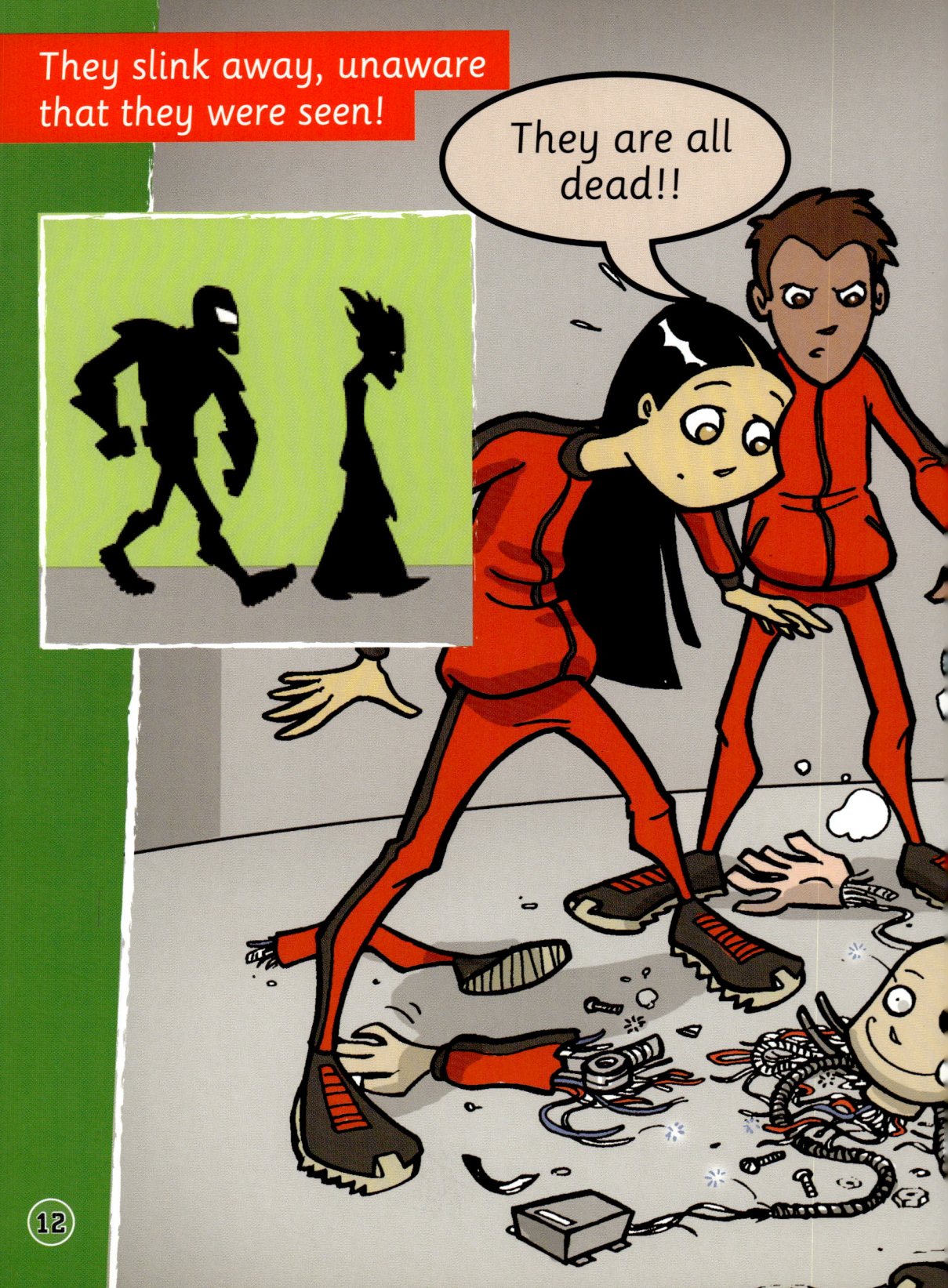

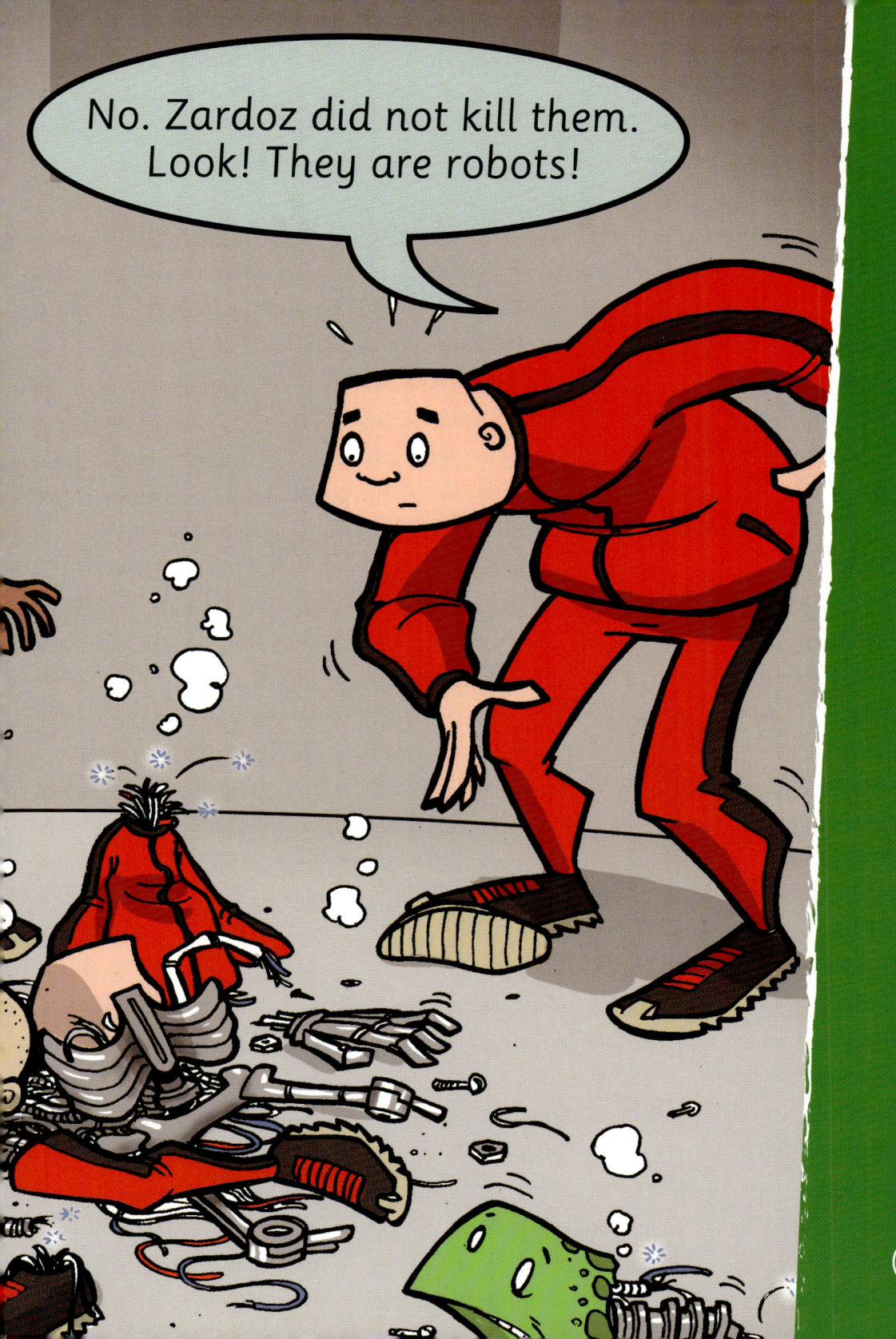

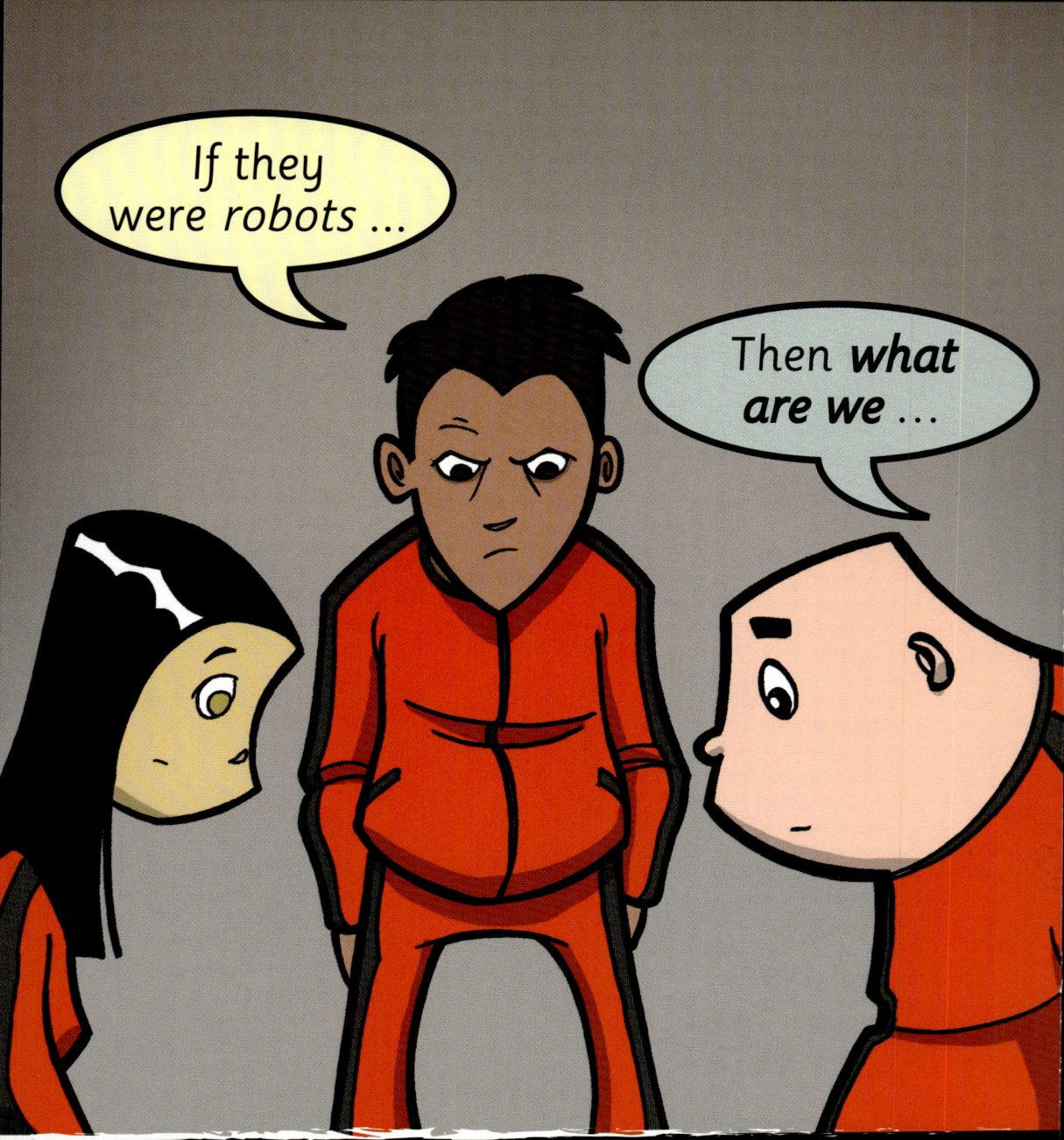